NO COMPLAINTS

How to Stop Sabotaging Your Own Joy

Cianna P. Stewart

Published in San Francisco, CA, USA

The No Complaining Project
www.GoNoCo.com

Editing by Darcie Clemen, Gail Fay, Kim Carr
Cover by Rich Black
Book design by Alan Barnett
Author photo by Bart Nagel

Any Internet addresses, phone numbers, or company or product information printed in this book are offered as a resource and are not intended in any way to be or to imply an endorsement by the publisher, nor does the publisher vouch for the existence, content, or services of these sites, phone numbers, companies, or products beyond the life of this book.

Library of Congress Control Number: 2017917887

ISBN 978-0-9996376-0-9

Printed in the United States of America

For my Dad,
who taught me early on how to see
from multiple perspectives

CONTENTS

Contents

Contents

INTRODUCTION

About ten years ago, I got sick of my own complaining and decided to stop. I thought it would be easy. I was wrong. What followed was a journey of research and self-discovery that had greater impact on every aspect of my life than I thought possible.

Since then I've been teaching people what I learned, and I've discovered that taking on the Practice of No Complaining—what I call Going NoCo—can be one of the most life-changing and beneficial things anyone can do.

Going NoCo changes how you move through the world and interact with others. It means that you are tired of being negative or stuck and are ready to take steps to change that. Going NoCo is not just for you—it will affect your relationships with everyone around you.

You'll move from feeling stuck to taking action. You'll learn tools to support difficult conversations and navigate change. You'll recognize why certain situations are emotionally charged and make decisions on how to handle them.

Go NoCo and see how much you can transform your world!

Who Is This For?

Going NoCo is for anyone who has been told that they're too negative and is ready to change but doesn't know where to start.

This is for anyone in a long-term relationship that somehow got filled with nagging, complaining, and sniping at each other.

This is for anyone in an imbalanced relationship in which one person feels like he or she is always being asked to support the other person, and it's exhausting.

This is for people who are unhappy at work. Negativity leads to higher turnover, lower productivity, and employee dissatisfaction. You know this isn't good for anyone but don't know how to turn things around.

This is for anyone who feels stuck and wants to make a change.

As a society, we are stressed out. More people are taking psych meds than ever before. Our levels of anxiety and depression are through the roof. We're sleeping less and working more, and despite all the comfort and conveniences of modern society, we just don't feel happy. We are bombarded by information and need a simple place to start.

Going NoCo is for you.

My Backstory

I didn't set out to rid the world of complaining. At the beginning, I was just sick of myself and my own attitude. Little did I know I was making a pledge that would forever change my life for the better.

It was 2006. I was well on the path to recovery from a devastating breakup that had cost me a lot financially and far more emotionally. After months of depression, I was finding my footing again. My friends were supporting me. I landed a job with someone who would become my mentor. And I was back home in San Francisco, living in a place that I love.

Things were going well. And yet I couldn't let go of my pain. Even though my current circumstances were great, I constantly complained about how much I had lost, what I had given up. My day would go well and I'd focus on what went wrong. I would laugh when I was together with my friends and then immediately slump back into a dark place as soon as I was alone.

One day I had an epiphany. I was driving along the freeway to my new job with my new mentor in my dream industry. I was remembering the dinner I'd cooked the previous night for my best friends in their home, where they invited me to stay as long as I needed. As I crested a rise in the road, I saw the San Francisco skyline bathed in a beautiful morning light, and my heart swelled with joy at being back in the Bay Area.

I suddenly realized that things were going very well for me—and that I hadn't noticed!

My brain instantly replayed the previous evening's conversations. When my friends complimented my cooking, I replied by complaining about not having my own kitchen any more. The memory of my reply shocked me. I then mentally scanned through other recent conversations and heard myself whining and complaining, throwing negative comments into every situation. I was horrified to realize how ungrateful I'd been to the people who were reaching out to help me. And I realized how much power I was still giving to my ex, letting that breakup continue to overshadow what I had right in front of me. I was living a life that could fill me with joy every day—but I was actively sabotaging that with my attitude.

I had a little fight with myself in the car and declared that I was no longer allowed to complain. It sounded pretty straightforward, and I was sure that I'd have no problem following this new rule. Boy, was I wrong!

A three-year journey of self-discovery, research, and a lot of trial and error followed. At first my impulse to complain was so strong that I often opted to just shut up. I then started to notice how many people around me complained and how often people complained about others' complaining. It seemed no one liked it, but everyone did it. My nerdy brain was intrigued.

I started taking classes and reading books about psychology, communications, relationships, group dynamics, management, habits, neurology, leadership, mindfulness, behavioral science—anything and everything that I thought might contribute to understanding how we communicate with each other and why we get triggered into saying things that we don't like to hear from others.

After one year, my own complaining was generally under control. After three years, I had a clear understanding of complaining in general and the interpersonal dynamics that contributed to it. I called my decision to stop complaining a "practice" because it required a daily commitment, and I developed heightened awareness and skills over time.

Seeing the positive effects that Going NoCo had on my relationships and on my own well-being, I started telling others what I'd done. After trying it on their own, friends told me they also found it difficult to quit complaining and asked me to teach them what I'd learned.

For the past several years, I've led workshops and written quite a bit about different aspects of complaining, how to break the habit, and what makes quitting difficult to do (see: GoNoCo.com). People have credited NoCo with improving their relationships, generating success at work, and helping lift the clouds of depression and anxiety.

This process always takes work, and I can't predict where it will lead you. I can say that you will learn many things as you journey from complaining to taking action. And if you're like me and the many others who have taken on this practice, Going NoCo will change your life for the better.

What You'll Find in This Journal

This journal contains prompts that will guide you through the process of breaking the complaining habit. It follows a well-established system for transforming habits that I refer to as AIR: Awareness, Interruption, Replacement.

In *Section 1: Getting Set Up*, you'll learn what is and is not a complaint. You'll identify what you need to set yourself up for success, and you'll assess your starting baseline.

In *Section 2: Awareness*, you'll learn the structure of complaints, learn why they're hurtful, and identify when and why we complain. This section gives you a deeper understanding of the emotions and patterns that underlie unconscious and habitual complaints.

In *Section 3: Interruption*, you'll receive internal and external tools that will help you interrupt these patterns. You'll learn to identify what makes it hard to keep your own resolutions, and be introduced to new ways of thinking.

Lastly, in *Section 4: Replacement*, you'll practice doing things that reinforce healthy patterns to make the change last. Going NoCo is a practice, not a one-time magic pill. The world will always present you with challenges and hardship. The trick is to build up good habits that will make you more resilient when difficulties arise.

Outside the Journal

While this journal is designed to stand alone, fuller explanations and examples to help clarify each step are available through the *No Complaints* podcast. It is designed to be a companion on your journey.

More resources are available on GoNoCo.com and Facebook.com/NoComplainingProject.

Thank you

On behalf of everyone you come into contact with and your future self, I thank you for deciding to take this journey.

Go NoCo!
— Cianna

"What you're supposed to do when you don't like a thing is change it. If you can't change it, change the way you think about it. Don't complain."

—Maya Angelou

GOING NOCO TAKES COURAGE
A MANIFESTO

The decision to stop complaining is not an easy one. When we take on the practice of No Complaints, we are doing much more than silencing negative conversation.

Going NoCo means:

We choose a new way of being in the world.
We challenge the culture of negativity.

We have decided to be agents of change in our own lives.
We are not observers passing commentary on the events of our lives without taking action.

We recognize and respect the impact we have on others.
We refuse to spew negativity at those around us.

We are willing to have hard conversations.
We refuse to hide when we're upset.

We are taking responsibility for our lives.
We refuse to blame others.

We recognize our own value.
We will not allow ourselves to be torn down, not even by our inner critic.

We strive for true connection.
   We refuse to bond at the expense of others.

We are willing to listen.
   We challenge the ways we are self-centered.

We are willing to live in reality.
   We have decided not to live in a fantasy world of perfection.

We are here now.
   We let past aggravations stay in the past.

We have gratitude for what is.
   We do not dwell on what isn't.

We are stepping into vulnerability and opening our hearts.
   **We have decided to stop hiding how we've been hurt
   and building walls to protect ourselves.**

We are willing to lead.
   We are not passively waiting for things to change.

Going NoCo takes courage.

Going NoCo means *we are ready to be fully alive.*

*For a free, print-ready PDF of the NoCo Manifesto,
go to GoNoCo.com/BookBonus*

SECTION 1
GETTING SET UP

Learn what is and is not a complaint

Assess your starting baseline

Identify what you need to set yourself up for success

1   What Is (and Is Not) Complaining?

The current dictionary definition of complain is "to express grief, pain, or discontent."

This definition is inadequate. In daily language we have a clear distinction between "filing a complaint" and "being a complainer" that isn't reflected here. We all need to say what's wrong to get things changed, to assert ourselves and our needs. But when we describe someone as "such a complainer," we mean something more than simply, "they express discontent."

After years of listening to and analyzing the structure of complaints and their impact, I have a new working definition.

Complain: To express grief, pain, or discontent without contributing to resolving the issue.

Complainers do not want to hear solutions. Even if the issue is something that could be addressed, they grumble to someone who can do nothing to help.

Habitual complainers repeat themselves without taking action. This is exhausting.

Using the preceding definition, I distinguish problem-solving from complaining, because problem-solving seeks to resolve the issue. Even if the words are the same, there's a fundamental difference between expressing discontent without intending to act and expressing a grievance directly to someone who can do something about it or who can help figure out what to do.

I make another key distinction between complaining and venting. Sometimes an incident and its related emotions are so current and overwhelming they distract you from paying attention to a current conversation. It can be important to share what's on your mind so that you and the person you're with have a mutual understanding of what each is thinking. This is venting. Sometimes, without this, it's difficult to be present. The key here, though, is that this can happen only once. If you repeat the issue at another time or to another person, that's complaining.

1

The intention of problem-solving is to resolve the issue.

The intention of venting is to have a shared reality so you can connect.

The intention of complaining…well, that's covered in the rest of this book.

The goal of taking on a No Complaining Practice (a.k.a. Going NoCo) is to move away from unhealthy complaining and toward resolving the issues in your world.

Using the new definition of complaining, write a list of things you often complain about. Who are you usually talking with?

My husbands health habits

my husband never wanting to spend time c me

My weight

Sitting too much

Not completing the tasks I want too.

Pictures aren't sorted

Cant sew

House isn't the way I want

Too much debt

Simone's too wild

Sick of freezing my butt off

Complain to/at my husband the most

11

2   Recognizing Micro-Complaints

Most of the time when we're thinking about our own complaining, we recall larger complaints, the kind that have some emotional weight. In contrast, when we're listening to others, we hear all their minor gripes and micro-complaints.

Examples of micro-complaints:

• Saying "I'm cold" without putting on a jacket

• Grumbling about a show on TV without changing the channel

• Looking at something and declaring it "a dumb design" and moving on

• Repeating "traffic sucks" on a daily commute

• Moping about being out of shape, and then settling in on the couch

• Declaring "I hate how this place has changed" and staying

If you want a complete picture of how others perceive you and how they relate to you, develop an awareness of your own micro-complaint habits.

Over the next few days, pay attention to your micro-complaints and make a list. How many of these are habitual? Who do you express them to?

2

"*There is a difference between really being concerned about service delivery and incompetence and just complaining for the sake of it.*"

—Zelda la Grange

3	What Do You Want to Change? And Why?

As you take on the practice of Going NoCo, you may find it gets difficult. You may want to quit halfway—after you've seen negative patterns but before you've been able to make lasting change.

By clearly articulating your goals before you start, you'll greatly increase your chance of success. Then, should things get tough, you can look back and focus on these goals, reminding yourself why you've decided to do this.

What do you want to change about the way you're living now?

Why do you want to make these changes?

3

Who would be affected if you make these changes?

If you make these changes, what will your life be like one year from now? Include as many details as you can.

17

4   Who Influences You?

Numerous studies have shown that the people we spend the most time with—and identify with—strongly influence our habits. Everything from how we dress to whether or not we smoke or exercise can be predicted by looking at the habits of the people around us.

It's not impossible to do something different from your crowd—but it is harder.

It's helpful to consider who has influence over your habits, and anticipate if your efforts to Go NoCo are likely to be supported or resisted.

Create a list of the people you spend the most time with and the people you're closest to.

Create a list of people whose opinions matter to you. How would you describe these individuals? For example: helpful, encouraging, critical, stubborn, passionate, bored, athletic, hardworking, easygoing, ambitious,…?

4

What do you admire about them?

How are you similar to or different from them?

SECTION 2
AWARENESS

Learn the structure of complaints

Learn why complaints are harmful

Identify when and why we complain

Gain a deeper understanding of the emotions and patterns
that underlie unconscious and habitual complaints

5   Complaining Compares Reality to Something Else

Nearly every complaint can be rewritten as "I wish reality wasn't happening." Think about how absurd that is. You live in this world, in this time, and in this body. Wishing alone won't change that.

Recognizing this pattern reveals what you wish was happening instead. This is useful. Understanding what you're using for comparison can point the way toward something worth pursuing.

Think about one of your ongoing complaints. What reality are you wishing for instead? Describe it in as much detail as you can.

Are any of those details things you can start making real? What would it take?

5

If you are in a situation that can't be changed, what can you do instead that would give you the feeling you're looking for?

6   Complaining Doesn't Invite Solutions

Sometimes we think we're "just getting things off our chest" or that we're doing something useful (a.k.a. problem-solving) when we're really complaining.

To test what your true intentions are, see what happens when your listener tries to offer a solution. Do you consider their suggestions or do you dismiss them? Are you hanging on to your original feelings or are you willing to let them go?

If you refuse all offers of help or bat away every suggestion, you are complaining. *

Think of a time when you were complaining to someone and he or she tried to offer help or solutions. What was your response?

* Note: In some situations, people refuse practical solutions because they seek emotional support instead. These individuals are still problem-solving. The difference is that the problem to be solved is their emotional state. Practical solutions are refused because they are not directed at the right thing. If you're the one who needs support, learn to ask for that directly. If you're the one listening, make it a practice to ask questions and have a full understanding of what's needed and what's already been tried instead of jumping in with solutions right away.

6

If you refused that person's help, how could you have responded differently?

7   Complaining Is Resistance or Avoidance

Often when we think that something can't be changed, we really mean that we're not willing or ready to do what it would take to change.

In this way, complaining can help us identify what we're resisting or avoiding, whether it's a change we're not willing to make or a tough conversation we're not willing to have.

Think of one of your most painful/entrenched complaints.

What change would you have to make in order to resolve this problem?

What gets in the way of you making that change?

7

What would you need to overcome this obstacle?

Can you imagine another way to resolve this problem that doesn't have this obstacle? Or is this a situation you need to walk away from?

8   Complaining Makes You Sound Like a Powerless Victim

Remember the NoCo definition of complain:

To express grief, pain, or discontent without contributing to resolving the issue.

When you complain and take no action, you send a message that you don't believe you are empowered to make a change. Over time, you sound as if you believe you are victimized by circumstance, that you feel powerless within your own life.

Think back on your frequent complaints and choose one. Write it here, why it bothers you, and what you wish happened instead.

How could you do things differently to avoid or minimize this issue? Create as long a list as possible; include things that feel impossible or ridiculous. (It's helpful to start each sentence with "I could…")

8

Which actions could you do now or soon? Did you list anything that you might be able to do with some help? With whose help?

"The secret lies not in avoiding life's inevitable frustrations and upsets but in learning to recover from them."

—Daniel Goleman

9 Habitual Complaining Hurts People Who Care About You

We often complain to people who care about us. We consider them a source of support and depend on them to hear us out.

Because they care, these people don't want us to suffer. They offer solutions and support. But if we're stuck on complaining and never take action, leaning on these people again and again can take its toll. The more empathetic they are, the more they absorb our pain.

If this continues, the people who care about us are left with two bad options: They can continue to feel pain at seeing us suffer, or they can protect themselves by hardening their hearts a little and caring a little less.

This is how chronic complaining eats away at caring relationships.

Think about the people around you who complain a lot. What is your response to their complaints? How do you feel after spending time with them?

9

Now think about those you complain to. How do you imagine your complaining is affecting that relationship?

10   Complaining Hurts Your Health

If you are a habitual complainer, you might repeatedly go over the same complaint, again and again, pulling down your mood and the moods of those around you.

While psychology hasn't studied habitual complaining directly, many studies have been done on rumination—and the definition is remarkably similar to complaining:

Rumination is the focused attention on the symptoms of one's distress and on its possible causes and consequences, as opposed to its solutions.

Rumination has been linked to depression, stress, and anxiety. These, in turn, are linked to substance abuse, eating disorders, and impaired problem-solving. Rumination can impact sleep and our cardiovascular health.

Pulling yourself out of habitual complaining can benefit your physical and mental well-being.

Where do you find yourself getting caught in a loop? Are there particular complaint topics or situations or stories that you find yourself revisiting again and again?

If you catch yourself repeating a complaint (even internally to yourself), take a moment to stop and observe yourself.

10

What are you focusing on? What are you feeling in your body?

Are you alone or with others? What happened right before you started thinking about this topic?

Are there other times/people/places that trigger these thoughts?

What would need to happen to resolve the issue?

11   Complaining Is Self-Absorbed

By definition, complaining doesn't involve searching for a solution, so the person listening to your complaint can't help solve the problem. If you're like many complainers, you probably repeat your complaints multiple times to different listeners, which shows that most of your complaints are not about having a conversation at all.

Complaining is essentially a monologue. It's one-sided. More often than not, complaining creates a distance between you and your listener—you are talking and the other person is just a prop. Even if you feel better by complaining, your listener rarely (if ever) does; he or she doesn't feel included in the conversation. Remember, listeners have rights, too.

Think about times when someone was complaining to you. (This is most acute when someone complains to you frequently.) Did you feel closer to that person afterward?

11

Now think about someone you complain to frequently. How do you think that person feels while you're complaining?

"The paradox is that although the drive behind excessive self-focus is to seek greater happiness for yourself, it ends up doing exactly the opposite. When you focus too much on yourself, you become disconnected and alienated from others."

—The Dalai Lama

12   Complaining Narrows Your Attention and Reduces Creativity

Neurologically, we are wired to look for problems or danger. This was key to our survival as a species, and our brains have evolved around this focus.

Obviously, this is not the only way our brains work. We can also be creative and joyful and loving.

What is true is that we find it easier to access thoughts related to whatever we think about more frequently. We can train our brains through conscious attention.

Frequent complaining keeps our attention on the negative, and studies have shown that this narrowed attention makes it more difficult to access creativity and learning.

Think of a time when you and others were negative and complaining a lot. Then think of a time when you were creative and came up with novel solutions to problems. Describe each.

12

What feelings did you experience in each situation? How were they different?

How might you turn a complaining group into a problem-solving group?

"We cannot feel good about an imaginary future while we are busy feeling bad about the present."

—Daniel Gilbert

13   Micro-Complaints Are More Damaging Than Large Ones

When we suffer a major physical injury, our immune system rallies all its resources to do what's necessary to heal our bodies as quickly as possible. If we have a minor injury or infection, our immune system sends out a much smaller response and sometimes we don't fully recover; we just get used to accommodating for the injury.

It turns out we have something like an emotional immune system that operates in much the same way. Studies have shown that we are generally more able to recover our overall mood after a crisis than in response to long-term, low-grade difficulties.

Micro-complaints—complaints about small, forgettable things—are like little irritants to our emotional immune system. They can lead to long-term suppression of our moods, our health, and our capacity for experiencing joy. Because we don't mount a full-scale response, we have a hard time recovering fully.

Keep track of the micro-complaints that you say throughout the day.

13

How do you expect others to respond when you express a micro-complaint? What are you hoping for?

Which of your micro-complaints could be transformed into a direct request for change?

14   The Culture of Complaining as Small Talk

In modern society, it's common to open conversations with a complaint. People arrive at a party and complain about the weather. They arrive at work and complain about the commute. They wake up and complain about feeling tired. People even arrive at a job interview and complain about whatever out of nervousness.

This kind of complaining is nearly unconscious, a collective habit, a social norm. Despite our desire to make a positive first impression, we start conversations by complaining and unintentionally paint ourselves in a negative light.

When you know you are going into a social situation, think in advance how you might answer standard questions like: How are you? What's been going on with you? How's work? How's the family? Be prepared with funny stories or interesting anecdotes that you enjoy discussing. What stories or topics come to mind when you think of approaching small talk in this way?

14

Another technique is to make small talk by asking questions. People generally enjoy talking about themselves, and it gets you away from the urge to complain.

For example, some of my favorites:
- What are you passionate about?
- What's something interesting that's happened to you in the past week?
- What are you curious about?
- Tell me something you're proud of.

15   Complaining to Bond

As human beings, we naturally feel kinship with others who have shared our struggles. This is so universal that it's become distorted into the common social habit of bonding through complaining.

This type of complaining reveals that we want to connect, that we're feeling alone in some way.

Think about a group you spend time with that complains together. What do you often complain about?

15

What connections do you have together other than complaining? How can you use these connections to have positive conversations? What else could you talk about or do?

16   Complaining to Get Attention

When someone complains in a group, all the attention turns to her or him. Given that speaking positively about yourself is considered "bragging," complaining has become the most culturally acceptable way of talking about yourself to get attention.

This type of complaining reveals that you are feeling overlooked.

When you catch yourself complaining to a group, think about the others who are there. What do you have in common with those people? What else could you talk about which would interest them and keep you involved in the conversation?

16

Do you enjoy complaining through telling funny stories? Think about the underlying message of what you're saying. Are you revealing that you're entitled or that you act superior? Are you tearing someone else down? Are you rehashing an old situation which is no longer relevant? Consider the message of your story and decide if that's what you want others to associate with you.

17 Complaining to Create Alliances

When we share complaints about another person or situation, we are unconsciously seeking allies. Complaining in this way asks, "Are you with me? Are you on my side in this?"

This kind of complaining comes up frequently when we feel threatened or fear loss of status in a hierarchy, such as at work.

Complaining like this reveals that we feel alone or at risk.

Describe a conversation in which you and someone else were complaining together about another person.

What do you gain by allying yourself with this other person?

17

How does it benefit you to criticize the target of your complaints?

What steps could you take to address the issues you raised in your complaints?

18   Complaining to Deflect Blame

When we are afraid of disappointing another person, we can slip into complaining about someone else's bad behavior or about circumstances "beyond our control." We say we missed a report deadline because the copier was broken. We arrive late for an event and berate the driver for getting stuck in traffic.

We complain like this in an effort to divert the blame away from ourselves and to avoid taking personal responsibility for actions we've taken that contributed to the outcome.

This type of complaining reveals a fear of retribution or loss of status.

Describe a time when you've disappointed someone and diverted the blame away from yourself.

Who or what did you complain about or reassign the blame to?

18

What did you believe would happen if you accepted full responsibility for your part in creating that outcome?

What could you have done instead that would have resulted in a different outcome?

"While amateurs complain, make excuses and blame others when their work doesn't work out the way they want it to, pros accept situations, take responsibility and own every situation that arises, good or bad."

—Paul Jarvis

19   Complaining to Deflect Compliments

Most of us find it difficult to accept compliments. We often use complaints to discharge this discomfort, for example, by referencing past failures or talking about how we didn't achieve what we intended.

When genuine, this type of complaining is usually a show of humility and a desire to not be elevated above another. It stems from a wish to stay connected with the person giving the compliment—but it has the opposite effect.

The person giving the compliment is offering appreciation, hoping for a moment of connection. However, the receiver's complaint has the effect of dismissing this. It's as if someone reached out a hand and had it batted away.

When we learn to receive compliments, we allow the person complimenting us to complete the gift they are trying to give, and we both end up feeling satisfied.

If someone does something you appreciate, share a compliment. How did that person respond? How did you feel afterward?

19

Think about someone who tried to give you a compliment or appreciation for something you did. How did you receive it?

Practice saying "thank you" after someone compliments you, and not adding to that. How challenging is this for you to do?

"We ask ourselves, who am I to be brilliant, gorgeous, handsome, talented and fabulous? Actually, who are you not to be?"

—Marianne Williamson

20	**Complaining to Feel Loved**

Some of us grew up in environments where we didn't get much caring affection unless we were sad or injured. Over time, we learned to associate complaining with getting love, and it became our go-to technique.

When we face situations that are emotionally difficult or that cause us extended physical pain, we can start complaining to get support—and this becomes a habit. Over time, others will find our complaints exhausting and start to pull away or minimize the amount of time they spend with us. This can make us feel even more isolated, which triggers more complaining, driving more people away.

This type of complaining often reveals that we are feeling neglected or unloved.

Have you found yourself listening reluctantly to a chronic complainer? If so, to whom? Imagine what it feels like to be that person. In what ways can you relate to his or her sense of isolation or need to feel loved? Can you find other ways to connect with this person?

20

Have there been times in your life when you became a chronic complainer? To whom did you turn? Were you able to maintain that relationship? What happened?

21   Complaining to Feel Superior

Tearing someone down when he or she is not around is often (consciously or unconsciously) an attempt to demonstrate superiority. This can take the form of malicious gossip, righteous indignation, or complaints. The triggers can be anything from feeling wronged or disrespected to simply feeling the need to demonstrate status, higher intelligence, or any other self-perceived superiority.

When we engage in this kind of complaining, we may feel better about ourselves, but our words can leave the listener with the opposite impression. We temporarily feel an alliance with our listener, but in actuality our words erode trust. The listener often comes away wondering if they could be the target of this verbal sniping when out of earshot.

In the end, we do not give off a powerful, superior impression. At the core, complaining about someone conveys an unwillingness to address problems directly, which only reinforces the perception of powerlessness.

When do you find yourself gossiping about others or criticizing people when they're not around? Who are you with? What is it about this situation that triggers complaints or gossip about others?

What would generate genuine respect for you with these people?

21

Think about the subject of your complaints and/or gossip. What keeps you from talking directly with this person about your concerns?

Imagine a conversation with the person you're criticizing. What do you need that person to hear and understand?

22   Complaining from Distorted Expectations

In modern Western society, we are bombarded with messages about how life should be and all the things we should have. Things that used to be difficult or out of reach are now taken for granted, and thanks to the Internet, we get 24/7 news about exceptional achievements and the very latest gadgets.

This distorts our expectations. We start to feel that we're behind if we don't have the latest/newest/fastest/best.

It's easy to forget that not everyone has the same access, particularly when we're surrounded by others who share our expectations. It's easy to feel disappointed and start complaining.

This type of complaining reveals a sense of entitlement.

When have you complained using phrases like "I don't deserve this treatment" or "I deserve better"?

Recognize these are moments when you felt entitled to something. What was it? Why do you feel that you are entitled to that (more than others)?

22

When you feel yourself becoming disappointed that something didn't meet your expectations, what is your response?

How else could you respond?

"You can't expand the volume of your chest just by sitting. You have to walk up mountains. There's a measure of going against, as it were, your nature. Your natural longing is to want to sit still. But if you do that and become a sofa cabbage or a couch potato, it's going to show. So what is true physically is, in a wonderful way, true spiritually as well. Deep down we grow in kindness when our kindness is tested."

—Archbishop Desmond Tutu

SPECIAL SECTION
THE INNER CRITIC

23   Complaining to Yourself About Yourself

For many of us, dealing with our inner critic is the greatest obstacle to self-confidence and peace of mind. In the context of NoCo, I've come to see the inner critic as a form of complaining about ourselves to ourselves. Like all other complaining, it's destructive if we do nothing in response—but can be helpful or useful if we use it as a catalyst for action.

Before we can take action in response to the inner critic, though, most of us need to find a way to soften its blows. One key is to try to understand what's underlying our internal complaints, what's driving them. For me and many I've worked with, the inner critic appears to primarily operate from a place of fear and protectiveness.

Most of the time, the inner critic works hard to be sure that we don't get cut out of the tribe. For example, because I long ago associated my value with my achievements, my inner critic tries to stop me from failing—whether repeating a past failure or doing something new without success. My old insecurities also show up as fear that others will leave me because I said or did something wrong.

My favorite technique for quieting the critic is to engage it in conversation. I recognize that my inner critic uses old information, is a slow learner, and has poor communication skills. I thank my inner critic for its concern, and say I'm grateful it's looking out for me. And then I remind it that I'm all grown up and have more skills than I used to. I remind my inner critic that I can't learn more without trying (and that trying means I'll sometimes fail). And I ask it to stop using such mean language.

Another technique for taming the inner critic is to use it as a tool for pointing out things you can learn. Most criticisms are rooted in something you fear or need to develop more skills to handle. Criticisms can reveal what matters to you.

23

What does your inner critic usually complain about? What could be driving those complaints?

If you were to have a conversation with your inner critic in which you asked for its compassion, what would you say?

What concerns does your inner critic have that you consider valid? How might you address those?

SECTION 3

INTERRUPTION

Gain internal and external tools
to interrupt habitual complaining

Learn to identify what makes it hard
to keep your own resolutions

Gain practical exercises to practice
new ways of responding

24   Consider Alternate Responses

We tend to think of events as causing our reactions and often treat our responses as if they are inevitable and the only option. But the truth is that the same event can result in different reactions in different people. Not only that, but the same emotion in different people can lead to different reactions.

By learning to recognize your own patterns and considering alternative ways of reacting, you'll gain greater choice in your responses to any situation.

Think of a frequent complaint in your life. What situation triggers your complaint?

24

Imagine different people in this same situation and their possible responses. For example, how would your best friend react? How would your favorite teacher react? How would Mary Poppins react? How would James Bond react? How would Serena Williams react? How would someone from a different country react? Add your own examples.

Considering all these different ways to react to the same situation, how else could you respond to this situation if it comes up again? How could you prepare for it?

*"We don't see things as they are,
we see them as we are."*

—Anais Nin

25   Establish NoCo Zones

Breaking the complaining habit is easiest when you bring others along with you on the effort. Designate certain locations or times to be No Complaining Zones.

Good areas to start with are the dinner table or the break room at work or your car.

Good times are the first 10–30 minutes after you or someone else gets home, during meals, or during meetings (focus on problem-solving instead).

What are situations in which you have influence over others? For instance: dinner time, a meeting you lead, at your desk, while you're driving, a team you coach.

Where will you institute your first NoCo Zone?

25

Who will join you in this effort?

For free, print-ready signage for NoCo Zones,
see GoNoCo.com/BookBonus

26   Assume You Don't Know the Whole Story

When we're complaining about someone's bad behavior, we often assume that person knew better and made a choice to do something we disagree with. In truth, we can't see inside someone's head and know all the things that are affecting his or her choices.

Most of us do things for a complex web of reasons. There are things we're trying to accomplish and things we're avoiding. There are people we want to impress and things we want to achieve. We can act out of insecurity or fear. We behave differently when we're tired or hungry or stressed.

Insert doubt into your complaints by imagining more complexity in the other person's behavior, knowing you're seeing just part of the story.

Describe a time when someone did something you thought they shouldn't have because they knew better.

What assumptions were you making about what that person knew?

26

What else could also be true? What could be beyond your perception that could have affected that person's choice of action?

What were your expectations? How did you communicate those expectations?

"*There are no right answers to wrong questions.*"

—*Ursula K. Le Guin*

27   Escape Complaint Spirals

Here's a familiar situation: A group of people are talking and one person starts complaining. Someone responds with a similar (or worse) complaint. Then the next person complains. And the next.

This a complaint spiral. One thing builds on another and another until the spiral has its own velocity that makes it hard to escape. (Note: This is especially powerful if anyone in the group is a skilled and/or funny storyteller.)

When you encounter a complaint spiral, challenge yourself to stop it by either naming it to the group or just introducing a new (positive) topic. If you can't stop the spiral, give yourself permission to leave the conversation. What happened when you tried to interrupt the spiral?

27

Who was in the group?

How did that group of people make it easier or harder to go against the spiral?

28   Consider Your Mood Before Entering

As a way of making small talk or checking in, we commonly complain soon after arriving in a new location or joining a group. Times when this is especially common include at home after work, directly after a meeting, after driving/parking/taking the subway, at a happy hour gathering, when we meet up with other parents, whenever we're nervous or tired.

To break this habit, take a pause before entering a situation. Notice the transition from where you were to where you will be. Breathe for a moment and settle your mind. Consciously choose your mood. Think of a topic of conversation that would be energizing and interesting for both you and others. Don't enter until you feel in control of your mood.

Where is your habit of using complaining as small talk the strongest?

28

How can you remind yourself to pause and consider alternative topics before entering that situation?

29   Remove Small Triggers

Entrenched complaints reveal that we're feeling stuck in parts of our lives, and it can be hard to overcome the inertia needed to tackle the issues that have us pinned down.

Experiencing small wins can kick-start the momentum necessary for larger change. When you don't have energy to tackle large projects, take care of minor things that annoy you, like sewing a button back on, greasing a squeaky hinge, cleaning a shelf, or filing papers.

Write a list of small annoyances and unfinished business.

29

Set aside time to resolve these little things. Try to do as many as possible. Cross them off the list and take a moment to appreciate finishing each one.

30   Look for What's Good, What's Working

We tend to see what we're looking for. While this seems obvious, we don't always stop and consider how what we decided to look for is affecting what we found. We forget how much our habits shape our worldview.

When we complain, we tend to see things that are wrong, and we reinforce this lens through more complaining. Over time, we have a hard time even noticing things that are good because all our attention is caught by what's wrong.

Do a hard reset by forcing yourself to look for things that are good in every situation. For example, in hard times you can think about the positive qualities of people around you, or congratulate yourself for sticking with it, or take stock of what you're learning as a result.

Even tough situations can have a good side—and sometimes it's simply that the situation isn't any worse.

What are some good things (large or small) in your life right now?

30

What is a situation that seems bleak right now? What are some good things inside that situation? What can you learn from it? If it's hard to come up with something, think about how the situation could be worse and practice being grateful that it's not.

"My mother would say to me, 'Look for the helpers. You will always find people who are helping.' To this day, especially in times of disaster, I remember my mother's words, and I am always comforted by realizing that there are still so many helpers—so many caring people in the world."

—Fred Rogers

31   Break Down Complex Systems into Parts You Can Affect

Complex systems can seem too big or too difficult to change, such as the government, our financial situation, our relationships, chronic health conditions, the state of the planet, and many more. This can lead to feelings of frustration, being demoralized, and complaining.

If we always think about the entire system, we can feel insignificant and powerless to change it. It's important to remember that complex systems are made up of many smaller parts, and these parts may be easier to change. If you focus your efforts on these parts, you can start to experience the small wins that add up to feeling more empowered. Over time, you can tackle bigger parts. Also over time, the cumulative effect of many small changes can lead to major change.

Identify one thing that frustrates you that seems too big or complicated to change. List as many things as you can that are parts of this complex system or that contribute to keeping it in place.

31

Look at your list and circle three things that are at a scale you can affect. If everything on the list seems too big, try breaking each thing down further until you get to a scale that feels manageable.

What is the first step you could take to address this?

32   Learn to Interpret Your Body's Signals

A common misperception is that we feel an emotion that leads to a physical response, such as thinking that embarrassment causes the face to flush. The truth is that the physical sensations happen first, and then our brain interprets them as an emotion. The same physical sensations can be interpreted in different ways. For instance, your face flushes. You might interpret this as embarrassment or as eagerness. Your stomach clenches, and you can interpret it as fear or exhilaration (or bad cheese).

When you are triggered, your body sends you a signal. If you can learn to identify that physical sensation, you can anticipate your own unconscious complaining and put a halt to it.

Find a quiet place to do a body scan. Put your attention on the top of your head and get curious about how the top of your head feels, what sensations are there. Drop your attention a few inches and see how the back of your head feels. Now your forehead. Now your ears. Keep doing this all the way down your body to have a mental picture of how your body feels at this moment. Now imagine something that brings you joy. Where in your body did you feel that? What changed about how your body felt?

32

Now imagine something that frustrates you or makes you angry. Where in your body did you feel that? What changed about how your body felt?

Try to remember this sensation linked to anger/frustration and be aware if you start to feel it. It may signal that you're open to complaining.

33   Reduce Depletion

When our lives become more complicated and we take on more responsibilities, our ability to control our emotions diminishes, our decision-making skills suffer, and our capacity for empathy decreases.

This reaction is amplified by the constant onslaught of information all of us encounter every day, each thing demanding a little of our attention. By the end of an overfull day, we are depleted, leaving us more open to irritation, less able to respond thoughtfully, and more prone to complaining.

For nearly all of us, some of our daily activities were actively chosen, while others became habits when we weren't paying attention. You can take back control over your energy by consciously crafting your day, balancing out depleting activities you must do with nourishing activities that keep you going.

In what aspects of your life do you face many decisions or demands on your attention? How much time do you spend daily on each?

What nonpersonal things take your attention on a daily basis, such as social media or the news? About how much time do you spend daily on each?

33

Looking at these areas, which are the priorities? Which are worth spending your energy on? (If any leave you feeling replenished, add a star.)

In which of these priority areas could you reduce the number of decisions you need to make by introducing a checklist or a routine? What would that look like?

How can you simplify or let go of the areas you identified as lower priority? (Keep as many starred items as possible.) Who might be able to help you with this?

" 'Crazy-busy' is a great armor, it's a great way for numbing. What a lot of us do is that we stay so busy, and so out in front of our life, that the truth of how we're feeling and what we really need can't catch up with us."

—Brené Brown

34   Stop Complaining to the Choir

Often when we complain to people who already agree with us about situations we want to change, we are not contributing to changing anything. We are reiterating information they already have and reinforcing our mutually established point of view. This is a common habit among long-time friends, political allies, work colleagues, parents, and many others with shared interests.

At first this is bonding, but over time, reiterating our common gripes without taking action simply focuses everyone on what hasn't changed and becomes demoralizing.

If we are serious about wanting to make a change, we must move these conversations away from complaining and toward action.

When you find yourself complaining to people who already agree with you, what topics do you collectively complain about?

34

Who are you with? Why do you complain in this way to these people? What do you gain from it?

How might you turn these conversations into strategy sessions where you share ideas about how to address the issue(s) at hand?

"I always wondered why somebody doesn't do something about that. Then I realized I was somebody."

—Lily Tomlin

35   Seek Out New Perspectives

Training ourselves to step outside of our own points of view and see alternatives leads to greater empathy, understanding, and creativity in finding solutions.

We can do this on our own or ask for help from the one who's listening to our complaint. That person can bring a different viewpoint on the reasons that something happened or offer alternative ways to respond.

Think of a specific situation in which you had a difference of opinion from another person. From your point of view, what happened?

Retell the story in the third person as if you were an objective security camera. Keep it to a simple string of facts, removing all interpretations and emotions.

35

Retell the story from the other person's point of view.

Now return to your own point of view. How else could you interpret what happened?

"How wonderful that we have met with a paradox. Now we have some hope of making progress."

—Niels Bohr

36   Use Judgments to Understand Your Fears

Our most heated judgments about others are rooted in things that we are uncomfortable about or are resisting within ourselves. Without our own internal discomfort, others' behavior does not trigger a strong emotional response.

Our complaints about others can help us recognize unresolved issues within ourselves.

What recurring judgments do you have about others? What is it about their behavior that triggers your complaints?

36

What is the origin of this judgment? What are you believing they should or should not know/do/say?

Imagine this judgment being passed on you. What is your response?

SECTION 4
REPLACEMENT

Start doing things that reinforce
patterns you want to maintain

Develop good habits that will
make you more resilient

37   Take Personal Responsibility

In every interaction between two people, each person plays a part in what happens. Often we argue "It's all your fault" or "You made me" or "I had no choice." The truth is, each person contributes to the outcome.

One of the single most powerful choices you can make is to take full responsibility for your actions every day with every person.

You can't control another person's behavior, but you can control your own. Once you take 100% responsibility, you unlock your ability to change your world.

Think of a specific situation with another person that you found difficult, frustrating, or exhausting. What happened?

How did you contribute to the outcome?

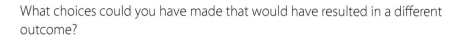

37

What choices could you have made that would have resulted in a different outcome?

What got in the way of making those choices?

How can you remind yourself in the future to remember all the choices you have available to you?

38   Imagine They Want the Best for You

In a crowd of strangers, it's common to imagine others are looking at you and having negative, judgmental thoughts. This is one of the main reasons so many people are uncomfortable in groups.

The truth is, you have no idea what anyone is thinking. So why not imagine positive things? There's even a term for it: pronoia. Pronoia is the suspicion that people are conspiring to help you or are wishing you the best. Give it a try!

As you go through your day, imagine that the people you encounter are wishing you well and that they want the best for you. When you have this mind-set, how do you feel about being around those people?

38

39   **Cultivate Daily Gratitude**

Just about every religious and spiritual tradition includes the practice of gratitude. There's good reason for it. Gratitude reminds us of our interconnectedness and of all that makes it possible for us be alive in this moment.

In our modern world, gratitude is important for pulling us out of the self-focused achievement and competition cycle. It's particularly useful as an antidote to complaining. We can use a gratitude practice to force ourselves to seek out the good in any moment.

Many people think that taking on a gratitude practice is limited to setting aside time to think deeply about our lives and sink into the feelings of gratitude for significant events and people in our lives. That practice is great and enriching, but it's not the only way. A gratitude practice can include focusing on the small events and things you notice as you go about your day and allowing yourself to feel gratitude in that moment.

Choose daily times and/or activities that you already do to which you can hook a moment of gratitude. Some examples:

When you wake each morning, take a moment to feel gratitude for having another day. As you're brushing your teeth, allow yourself feel gratitude for the things around you that happen without you having to consciously make them happen.

If you're having trouble thinking of things, you can start by considering your heart, which beats continually without any help from you. Then you can expand to include any water you use that you didn't have to go to the source to get, any electricity you use that you didn't have to generate. As you step outside your house, look around and feel gratitude for all the people who have contributed to your life without your involvement, such as those who grew and transported the food you eat, and those who planned and paved the streets around you.

When are good times for you to pause for a moment and allow yourself to feel gratitude? What can you use to remind yourself to do this practice?

39

"Someone is sitting in the shade today because someone planted a tree a long time ago."

—Warren Buffett

40   Set Aside Time Without Inputs

Modern society bombards us with information and sensory inputs nearly every minute of every day. With so many things competing for our attention, we absorb the message that we need to keep up and do more to avoid falling behind.

This constant barrage has a real cost. It increases our stress levels, raises anxiety, and keeps us depleted. It decreases our decision-making abilities and our creativity levels.

To counter this, set aside time every day to be in silence without any inputs. Allow yourself to get bored without trying to fill the space.

We can benefit from just 5–10 minutes of silence a day without any goals, without listening to or reading or watching anything. This doesn't have to be a formal meditation (although that's great if you can do it). You can start by not listening to music or podcasts when you're walking or driving, or by not picking up your phone to distract you when you're waiting in line.

Where in your day can you find five minutes to be in silence?

40

Is being silent easier for you to do sitting or walking?

What thoughts keep coming up when you're being silent? Have they changed as you've continued this practice?

41   Seek Out Opportunities to Give

One of complaining's defining characteristics is the focus on self. This can be counteracted by consciously seeking out opportunities to give to others.

Generosity is highly valued around the world. Through giving, we connect and strengthen our bonds with other people. We are reminded that we are an interdependent species, our lives intertwined with others from the moment we are born.

When we give, we trigger the release of endorphins in our brains, which can reduce pain and cause euphoria. The more we are able to give with a generous heart—giving without expecting reciprocal receiving—the more we build up trust with others.

Think about the resources you have available. Think beyond your material resources and include your experience, your caring, your skills, your time, your smile. Who could benefit from your resources? How could you give them your support?

41

Think about the people you frequently turn to for support. In what ways could you give to them? How could you support them beyond the support they have offered you?

"No one is useless in this world who lightens the burdens of another."

—Charles Dickens

42   Cultivate a Focus on Process

Many complaints stem from impatience and having a singular focus on a goal. We can't wait to get there, to finish, for this to be over already. We become so focused on the end that we don't appreciate (or even remember) the process of getting there.

At its extreme, this focus can lead to taking shortcuts or giving up when something becomes difficult. Studies have shown that levels of achievement and personal satisfaction both increase when someone has a higher level of grit or perseverance.

One way to cultivate grit is to develop an appreciation for small wins along the way, focusing on the effort and what you've learned from the process (including things you tried that didn't work).

Of course, focusing on effort can go too far and become unsustainable if you place all your attention on that alone. Valuing grit is not a justification for becoming a stressed-out workaholic. The idea is to have clear long-term goals and a healthy sense of pride in the effort you'll put in to achieve them, combined with enough play to recharge, the desire to learn new things, and a sense of gratitude for what you already have. That combination leads to a sustainable life of achievement and satisfaction.

Where do you find yourself getting impatient and focusing solely on outcome?

42

Where in the process of doing those things can you find moments to celebrate small wins?

Think about a time when you tried something that didn't work and you felt like you failed. Turn this around into an educational experience to benefit your future efforts. What did you learn that can inform the next time you try? What contributed to your giving up? What support would you need to keep going?

43   Cultivate Curiosity and Wonder

If you find yourself feeling "over it" or bored, this is a signal that your curiosity is not engaged. Seeking out new things—or new ways to think about familiar things—is fun. It's also good for your overall mood and health.

Curiosity is associated with lower levels of anxiety and increased life satisfaction. Learning to stay curious can deepen and enrich your relationships and increase empathy.

The phrase child-like wonder is a reminder that we all were curious once and that losing curiosity is associated with feeling old.

Cultivating curiosity takes little more than reminding yourself that you don't know everything about anything—no matter what it is or who you are—and then seeking out new information and experiences. Cultivating wonder simply means letting yourself feel awe when you see, learn, or experience something new.

Think of a topic that you know well, maybe one you're starting to get bored with. Imagine it with a new perspective from a different angle of study.

For example, when I go hiking out in the woods I can think about the surrounding beauty and how to photograph it, what it takes to maintain a trail, how someone found that trail in the first place, the trees and plants from a botanist's point of view, what a geologist would know about that location, how people who study birds or insects would see things I don't, how someone from a different culture might think about hiking, the body mechanics of walking, what it would have been like to hike this area before the 1800s, how different artists would paint it… The options are endless.

43

"For me, I am driven by two main philosophies: know more today about the world than I knew yesterday and lessen the suffering of others. You'd be surprised how far that gets you."

—Neil deGrasse Tyson

44   Use Language of Agency and Responsibility

Complaining assumes a perspective of passivity and disempowerment. For example, every time we say that we "have to" do something, we are subconsciously reinforcing that we don't have choice, as if we are not in control of our lives.

Our language is not just a reflection of how we feel; it can also shape our outlook and our moods. When we continually use passive language, we wear down our sense of agency. The good news is the reverse is also true.

Experiment with moving away from a language of powerlessness and passivity, and replacing it with active language to boost your feelings of choice and personal power.

Think of common sentences you start with "I have to." Replace that phrase with "I get to" or "I choose to" or "I will."

How does this affect how you perceive that activity?

44

How does this affect how you perceive yourself?

45   Remember to Play and Find Your Flow

There are certain activities for each of us that cause us to lose a sense of time. We enjoy ourselves so much that we do them without effort, sometimes only realizing later that our bodies are tired—while our minds are charged up.

Depending on the activity (and the person), this is referred to as play or being in flow or getting in the zone. Finding our flow is incredibly valuable for rejuvenating ourselves, being creative, reducing stress, and generally being satisfied with life.

What are the key qualities of flow? It's an active (not passive) activity with the right level of challenge, feedback is immediate, and the goals are clear. We don't achieve flow if we're doing it for external reasons. The activity must be intrinsically enjoyable to us.

Often when we complain that our life feels imbalanced, we are not consciously leaving time for flow or play activities.

What are some activities that leave you feeling energized, that reduce your stress, and that cause you to lose a sense of time and effort?

45

How often do you engage in these activities?

How might you make more time for these activities?

"*Men do not quit playing because they grow old; they grow old because they quit playing.*"

—Oliver Wendell Holmes Sr.

We often think of our bodies and our expressions as reflecting our thoughts and our moods, but the opposite is also true. We can use our posture and expressions to change our moods.

Studies have shown that certain facial expressions and body postures can trigger the release of brain chemicals. These, in turn, can affect our moods, making us feel happier or confident or insecure. For instance, smiling for twenty seconds can reduce the stress hormone cortisol and trigger the release of endorphins.

When we were young and adults told us to "stand up straight and smile," they were onto something.

Think of a situation in which you're being asked to do something difficult or that scares you.

Hunch your shoulders forward. Slump your chin onto your chest. Hold your knees together and make all your muscles tight. Frown. Imagine yourself facing that situation while you're in this posture.

Now stand or sit with your back straight. Push your chest out and your shoulders back. Smile. Put your hands on your hips. Take a few deep breaths and hold this posture for two minutes. Now imagine yourself facing that same situation while you're in this posture.

What differences did you experience between the two postures?

46

Practice doing the second posture any time you're thinking about something that is difficult or just before you go into any situation where you're feeling insecure.

Also, practice smiling for no reason as often as possible.

47 Practice the Mindfulness of Tiny Moments

Mindfulness is the practice of becoming aware of the present moment and bringing your full attention to it. It's the antithesis of the habit of complaining and comparing reality to something else.

Practicing mindfulness does not have to mean saving large chunks of time to meditate. You can practice becoming aware during small, ordinary moments.

Choose a time every day when you can take two minutes to practice bringing your full attention to the present moment. You can be doing anything, such as walking, or washing the dishes, or sipping coffee.

During that time, ask yourself questions such as: What am I seeing? What am I hearing? How does my tongue taste? What do I feel in my body? What am I noticing in this moment? And in this moment?

After a few days, ask yourself, what has changed about what I'm noticing?

47

"While drinking the cup of tea, we will only be thinking of other things, barely aware of the cup in our hands. Thus we are sucked away into the future—and we are incapable of actually living one minute of life."

—Thich Nhat Hanh

48   Use the Right Measuring Sticks

Many complaints arise from comparing ourselves to another person or a particular standard, and then deciding that we've fallen short.

Comparing ourselves to others is never a fair comparison. We are comparing our inner world (with all our insecurities and faults and failed intentions and guilt) to whatever that person presents to the outside world. We are comparing their end results with our process.

Of course, comparing ourselves to an external standard can be useful and motivating—if it's the right standard and if we've realistically made the kinds of commitments that are necessary to achieve it. For instance, I hear many people saying things like, "I would have been a great ____," without taking into account their own lack of commitment to the hours of practice it would have taken to achieve their imagined greatness.

You can counteract the impulse to make comparisons by pausing and reminding yourself of the assumptions you are making, the reasons you made certain choices in the past, and choices still available to you today.

Think of a situation in which you compared your life with another person's life. What assumptions did you make about what it feels like to be that person? What don't you know about being that person or living that life?

48

Think of something you've said that you wanted to do. What would it take to do that? What would you have to give up or change about your current life in order to do that? Are you willing to make those changes? If yes, start! If not, then allow yourself to let go of the idea.

Bonus: The next time you encounter someone who is doing that thing you've wanted to do, admire their level of commitment without making a comparison to yourself. Instead, appreciate the things that you've experienced with that extra time.

"It is impossible to escape the impression that people commonly use false standards of measurement—that they seek power, success and wealth for themselves and admire them in others, and that they underestimate what is of true value in life."

—Sigmund Freud

49   Practice Being Satisfied

Being a maximizer means always wanting to be sure that you made the very best choice in everything. In our world of endless choices, this can be paralyzing, leading to doubt, anxiety, and depression.

Research has shown that when we are given three options, we can decide more easily and are happier with our decision than when we are given more choices.

In today's world, we have seemingly endless choices in everything from snack foods to phone apps to career paths to whom we might date. It takes conscious effort to counteract the paralyzing and self-doubting effects of having so many options.

Instead of always going for the best, practice being clear on your criteria for choosing, deciding to quit the search when you've found something that fits, and being satisfied with your choice.

Where are you finding yourself spending too much time trying to decide between options?

Without thinking about the specific choices, write down what you would consider a good outcome of making this decision. (Note: The question is not what would be the best outcome?)

49

What are essential qualities of a good choice in this case? (It can be useful to remember the old adage, "Fast, cheap, or good. Pick two.")

Select three options that have these qualities. This narrowing down can be arbitrary. (Sometimes asking a friend to do it can help if you're still indecisive.) Choose from those three. Move on.

"We make the most of our freedoms by learning to make good choices about the things that matter, while at the same time unburdening ourselves from too much concern about the things that don't."

—Barry Schwartz

50   Practice Listening to Understand

Listening is a key skill for connecting deeply with another person, for fully understanding another's needs, and for building strong relationships in every aspect of life. Listening is very different from simply hearing the words that someone said; it means giving full attention to the speaker without constructing a response in your mind or tuning out until it's your turn to speak.

Make an internal commitment to practice listening to others without interrupting them. Have a goal of fully understanding them without judgment.

When you are listening to someone, give her or him your full focus. When the person finishes, repeat what's been said in your own words to confirm that you understood what was meant. You can start by saying, "What I heard you say is…" If you missed anything, ask the person to explain until you understand.

Practice holding back your own thoughts and responses until after you have a full understanding of the other person's perspective and intentions.

How might listening in this way affect certain interactions?

In what ways is this listening different from or similar to how you listen now?

Is this kind of listening easier or harder to do with certain people or in certain situations? Who and where?

"When people talk, listen completely.
Most people never listen."

—Ernest Hemingway

51 Practice Good Will

One of the more surprising ways to feel better is to consciously set aside time to wish others well. Most, if not all, religious and spiritual traditions include some form of this practice, whether it's called praying for others, or metta meditation, or something else.

When you devote your attention to others, you will be lifted out of a focus on yourself and your own suffering. Over time, you will gain an understanding that we all have struggles, that we are all connected, and that you are not alone.

This practice has been shown to sustain positive mental health and reduce depression.

Sit quietly with your eyes closed. Then send phrases or prayers for good will and health.

Traditional phrases from the Buddhist practice of metta meditation include: "May you be safe and protected," "May you be healthy and strong," "May you be free from suffering," and "May you take care of yourselves happily." In this practice, you include people you love, people you're neutral toward, people you have difficulty with, yourself, and all beings everywhere.

Christian traditions often ask God to watch over someone or an entire group of people. In this practice, you name each person or group and take a moment to bring them to mind as you pray.

Most other religious and spiritual traditions have a similar practice with their own traditional phrases.

You can use these approaches or any that come naturally to you. The key is to take a moment to think of each person or group of people in turn, and send them good will. If you mindlessly repeat this list, the practice has lost its meaning.

Note if there are changes in how you feel toward someone or areas in which it is more difficult for you to practice good will. What makes it easier/harder for you?

51

"You are alive today not because you want to be, but because the universe wants you to be."

—A. H. Almaas

52   Handle What You've Been Avoiding

Our most entrenched complaints revolve around situations and/or conversations that we've been avoiding. Moving away from complaining and toward taking action means having the courage to face our fears. Developing the skills and resources to handle difficult or uncomfortable situations is the true goal of Going NoCo.

This is the last lesson because it's a huge one. Often there's a good reason we've been avoiding addressing something. We may feel concern that we don't have the skills, knowledge, or support to tackle something difficult. Or we may not feel prepared to face the consequences of a hard conversation. There is great value in tackling what you've been avoiding, giving yourself a break if it feels hard, then getting up and trying it again.

Think about a difficult situation which you have not addressed directly even though it aggravates you. What action would you need to take in order to resolve this?

What is in the way of you taking this action?

52

What kind of support do you need in order to take this action?

Are you willing to take this action? What would make it worthwhile for you?

For a free worksheet to support breaking down difficult situations, see:
GoNoCo.com/BookBonus

"A person isn't who they are during the last conversation you had with them—they're who they've been throughout your relationship."

—Rainer Maria Rilke

CONGRATULATIONS
AND THANK YOU!

Thank you for giving this gift to yourself and to those around you.

Flip back to the beginning of this journal and re-read where you started. Take a moment to reflect on what you have accomplished and note where you still want to put your focus. Congratulations!

Now imagine how much more connected and joyful we would all be if everyone did this work…

In gratitude,
— Cianna

KEEP LEARNING AND GROWING

No Complaints emerged out of years of reading, conversations, and trainings, all of which drew on a wide variety of fields. I am deeply grateful to the teachers and researchers who have made their work available for the benefit of us all.

I highly recommend that you continue to learn and grow on your own. I will continue to post new resources on www.GoNoCo.com. Here are a few that I recommend starting with (in alphabetical order because there's no way to rank their impact on me):

Big Magic by Elizabeth Gilbert (2015). New York, NY: Riverhead Books.

The Book of Joy by His Holiness the Dalai Lama and Archbishop Desmond Tutu, with Douglas Abrams (2016). New York, NY: Avery.

Difficult Conversations: How to Discuss What Matters Most by Douglas Stone, Bruce Patton, Sheila Heen, and Roger Fisher (2010). New York, NY: Penguin Group.

The Gifts of Imperfection by Brené Brown (2010). New York, NY: Hazelden Publishing.

Give and Take by Adam Grant (2013). New York, NY: Penguin Group.

Meditation in Action by Chögyam Trungpa (2010). Boston, MA: Shambala.

The Paradox of Choice: Why More Is Less by Barry Schwartz (2009). New York, NY: HarperCollins Publishers.

The Power of the Positive No by William Ury (2007). New York, NY: Bantam.

Start Where You Are: A Guide to Compassionate Living by Pema Chödrön (2001). Boston, MA: Shambala Classics.

Stumbling on Happiness by Daniel Gilbert (2005). New York, NY: Vintage Books.

Thanks for the Feedback: The Science and Art of Receiving Feedback Well by Douglas Stone and Sheila Heen (2015). New York, NY: Penguin Books.

What Makes Love Last by John M. Gottman, PhD, and Nan Silver (2012). New York, NY: Simon & Shuster.

WITH GRATITUDE

How to thank all the people who have contributed to my journey over the past 10 years of working on The No Complaining Project? That's an impossible task. There is no way I would have come through this decade with its cycles of depression, recovery, excitement, purpose, wandering, and fun without everyone who listened to me, pushed me, questioned me, answered me, taught me, danced with me, and been my support. I thank all of you deeply.

To focus on those who have helped me overcome my self-created obstacles so this book could be finished:

My deepest gratitude in all things goes to my core circle: Jeanine Walters, Audrey Heller, Paul Bostwick, Tina Owenmark, Genevieve Buckley, Kendal Texeira, and my brother, Scott. You have been the axle as I spun, keeping me on track and making sure I always returned to center. I would not be who I am without you.

I owe so much to Vanessa Naylon for holding together the Goals Gals and me, and for ongoing support from Karen Nguyen and Shayla Smith. Thank you. I'm totally putting this down on my Accomplishments Card for Q4 2017!

The NoCo content has been tested, tweaked, and refined through workshops, provocative questions, and illuminating conversations. For the magic of live incubation, I am grateful to Mike Yuen, Toshi Hoo, Daniel Berkman, Moldover, Sophia Robinson, Dixie de la Tour, Joseph Pred, Elle Beigh, Jason Wallace, Sasha Yee, Deb Fink, Nina Ramos, Joe Zarate-Sanderlin, Tom Bozeman, Tim Kingston, Michelle Huston, Roxanne Gomez, Shing Kong, and all of Priceless.

For holding my writer's pen to the fire until the book was finished, a special call-out to David Hermele who pre-ordered the very first copy and then gently checked on delivery for 5+ years.

Marcia Baczyinzki: Thanks for making me pinky swear I'd finish! It's time for breakfast, and then I'll be lazy.

My beautiful, wonderful, sweet roommate, Penny Fellbrich: You are a daily inspiration. You've lived with this project for years now, and I always will learn from you!

My editors, Darcie Clemen, Gail Fay, and Kim Carr, wonderfully wrangled my wandering words and made them shine. If there's a confusing sentence or an errant word, the fault is entirely mine.

Rich Black is an amazing artist who beautifies everything NoCo. Thank you to Alan Barnett for the clarity of your design. Thanks to Jim Hicks for getting Mr. NoCo out from under that umbrella, and to Phillip Kim for making things people want to put on their wall.

For going beyond updating the website and into asking me the big questions I need to answer, I thank Kristin Long. Listener's Rights forever!

Joe Homs, Erin Firmat, Aly Ash, Paul Overton, and Tessa Auza told me stories which I hold dear and which continue to inspire me to do this work. Thank you. I needed that.

To the ex who catalyzed my depression and resulting NoCo epiphany: Thank you. I have concrete proof now that something good can be made out of anything.

TENCUE: You cheer me on and give me a greater sense of place than I imagined possible. Every one of you deserves the biggest praising stump in the world. Thank you for supporting my side projects and me.

For late night deep thoughts, early morning scrambles, and so much loving support while I obsessed on this book, I owe a debt of gratitude to Scott Kildall. Meow.

Thank you, Melody Stewart, for being steadily supportive and an inspiration on how to give just that much more. You blow me away.

Tita Ana, my aunt and my very dear friend: I feel deeply fortunate to have had as much time as we've had together. Now the book is done, let's take another trip!

And last on the list but first in my heart, thank you to my Dad. I've learned so much from you about how to think and how to be. I hope I make you proud.

ADDITIONAL RESOURCES

For more information:
GoNoCo.com or Facebook.com/NoComplainingProject

ABOUT THE AUTHOR

Cianna P. Stewart is the founder of The No Complaining
Project, where she's been studying the impact and mechanics
of complaining for over a decade, as well as writing and
leading courses on how to stop. Her varied resume includes:
Event production, directing theater, making documentaries,
HIV prevention, playwriting, nonprofit program design,
community organizing, and creating tiny hats for window
display mannequins. She really is super curious about nearly
everything. She doesn't complain very much anymore.
Tweet @cianna and visit www.gonoco.com to say hi.